THE CONTEMPLATIVE LIFE:
A CURRENT APPROACH

by

Sister Eileen Mary SLG

SLG PRESS
Convent of the Incarnation
Fairacres   Oxford

THE CONTEMPLATIVE LIFE: A CURRENT APPROACH

The nature of witness and of contemplative life

In common with other words of ancient and honourable lineage, the terms 'contemplation' and the 'contemplative life' have gathered around themselves a cluster of images, some more true to the Christian tradition than others. The meaning of the contemplative life, as it is understood by Christians, has to be disentangled from ideas of dualism, Platonism and perhaps even gnosticism which have entwined themselves around it at different stages of its history, ideas of great attractiveness to the natural mystic in man, involving as they do the separation and transcendence of matter by spirit and the acquisition of knowledge by techniques and disciplines.

Although it would be widely accepted today on an intellectual level that Christian contemplation must be concerned with the transformation of the whole of creation rather than by its transcendence, yet the way in which this has to be performed is as unpopular and difficult to the natural man as it ever was, and the temptation to replace it by philanthropic work or by some form of spiritual selfishness equally subtle and seductive.

Perhaps the true secret of the Christian contemplative life lies hidden in some words which Dostoievsky put into the mouth of the Elder Zossima in his book *The Brothers Karamazov:*

'Love in action is a hard and dreadful thing compared with love in dreams. Love in dreams is greedy for immediate action, rapidly performed, and in the sight of all. Men will even give their lives if only the ordeal does not last long but is soon over with all looking on and applauding as though on the stage. *But active love is labour and fortitude, and for some people too, perhaps a complete science.*'

For, above all, the contemplative life involves this science of love, the crown and completion of which is to be found in the life of the Beatitudes rather than in visions, which may or may not be given, but in any case are incidental to the way as it has to be followed in this life. The witness which the contemplative is called to give in and to the world is essentially one of hidden stability and warfare, corresponding to, and sometimes involving the witness of actual physical martyrdom. It affirms before God and the whole cosmos its belief in a truth of being and loving which sweetens and purifies the earth whether the world knows of the existence of the witness or not. In our day this essential witness is the same as it has ever been, whether it is lived within the traditional setting of a monastery or hermitage, or in places as far removed from each other as a council flat on a housing estate and a labour camp in Siberia. Today television and radio programmes may have made the existence of such a life better known, but still the true witness lies in the steady affirmation of faith and love in those hidden centres of life which in the spiritual realm are set against the powers of darkness which are continually seeking to draw the world wholly into their own orbit.

The way

If poverty of spirit, purity of heart, gentleness and peace-making and the other Beatitudes are marks of the contemplative life when lived in its fullness, it follows that all Christians must, in the widest sense, be called to follow this way, and that the ultimate ideals and disciplines which are enshrined in the ancient spiritual rules of the monastic life must in a variety of ways be expressed through the life of every Christian according to his or her vocation in the Church. The lives of the saints are infinitely various, infinitely rich, yet common to all is the acceptance, joy, courage and humility by which they are known. Their way more often than not is one of contemplative action and active contemplation in which salvation does not lie in the amount of moral effort made, nor penance endured nor silence and withdrawal practised, but in something more ontological, involving the whole man in his relationship to God, to the exterior world, and to that of his own inner being. Their lives involve an ability to discern and to respond creatively and appropriately to every manifestation of reality as it makes its demands upon them; they possess an inner sight and hearing which are themselves the fruit of this obedience, an acceptance which in its turn nourishes and increases a sensitivity of response to the calls of reality which are being made upon them at each moment of the day from the world without, from conscience within and from the challenge of other men.

Christ himself, in the Gospels, lays down the dividing line between those who have, and those who have not the power to see, hear and discern the mystery of truth which lies behind the parables of every-day life:

'To you it has been given to know the secrets of the kingdom of heaven, but to them it has not been given. For to him who has will more be given, and he will have abundance, but from him who has not, even what he has will be taken away. This is why I speak to them in parables, because seeing they do not see and hearing they do not hear, nor do they understand.' (Matthew 13:11-13 *RSV.*)

It is clear that a man is not faultless in the sight of God if he has either lost this power of discernment or been too occupied or frivolous to develop it:

'The eye is the lamp of the body. So if your eye is sound, your whole body will be full of light, but if your eye is not sound, your whole body will be full of darkness. If then the light in you is darkness, how great is the darkness.' (Matt. 6:22.)

The corn still grows in the field as it did when Jesus used it as a parable of human life, and that life still comes to every man in signs which he can be too engrossed to discern, too choked with the cares and anxieties and pleasures of this life to understand, or too worldly-wise even to notice. Yet those of an honest and true heart hear the word of God and keep it, and these are the contemplatives of the world whether they know themselves to be so or not.

The gateway to reality is narrow for every man and most of us shrink from the compression involved in passing through, trying in a multitude of ways to fit reality to ourselves, rather than ourselves to reality. Therefore it is too vague to talk of practising the Christian and contemplative life in a vacuum. For every Christian there is a particular gate of vocation involving disciplines which are not practised for the sake of gaining esoteric knowledge but because they represent for him the necessary narrowing of the way through which he must continually be passing if he is to meet inner and outer reality at a point. And so it is one of the primary functions of a contemplative community to witness through its enclosure and stability to this truth. Such a community is in one aspect of its life an experimental workshop in which the implications, laws and consequences of such a vocation are worked out for the Church and world as a whole, much as any scientist or artist works out truth in his own particular sphere, not primarily for himself but as his contribution to total mankind.

The 'vertical' witness of the contemplative community

All that has been said up till now has pointed the way to the basic necessity of incarnation, to a vision which must be clothed in the stuff of everyday life. This does not only include an individual relationship with God but also a whole pattern of human relationships which find their grass roots reality in the life of a family. In the Orthodox Church a priest is obliged to be married or to be a monk; his priestly function must be anchored in the reality of human life lived at its most intimate level, in an inescapable, permanent obligation in which 'love is labour and fortitude and . . . perhaps a complete science'. So, too, if an enclosed community is to realise its vocation to be a eucharistic centre of praise on earth, a place where God's glory is supreme, its members must experience the inevitable tensions as well as the joys of human life lived closely and inescapably together.

The German poet Rilke, although not a Christian, speaks with the voice of the contemplative as he witnesses to the truth that eucharistic praise must involve the whole of life:

> Tell us, poet, what it is you do. — I praise.
> But the deadly and monstrous things, how can you
>   bear them, how can you accept them? — I praise.
> But even what is nameless, what is anonymous, how can
>   you call upon it? — I praise.
> What right have you to be true in every disguise,
>   beneath every mask? — I praise.
> And how is it that both calm and violent things, like star
>   and storm, know you for their own? — Because I praise.[1]

So the central witness of the contemplative monastic life lies in the rhythm of liturgical worship performed seven times in the day and in the night, not for the edification of the Religious but as an affirmation and praise of all reality, offered as it is by a representative group of the whole family of the Church, and indeed of mankind, an affirmation of worship and trust in the belief that despite the darkness and mystery at the heart of the

---

1. This translation is taken from *The Penguin Book of German Verse*, p. 399, and is reprinted here by kind permission of the Executors of the Estate of Rainer Maria Rilke and the Hogarth Press.

universe, God reigns, is sovereign and supreme, and has made all things well. Thus the contemplative life witnesses to the reality of God.

It witnesses too, through its work of intercession, to the fact of the solidarity of all mankind in Christ and in Adam, to a unity of the human race which persists despite its fragility and frailty.

Mankind is like a great and ancient tree. Cut it across the trunk and one sees the circles which mark the years of its age. Look at its roots grounded deeply in the earth, in the natural, in the stuff of creation. Look at its leaves and branches outstretched to receive life and warmth and moisture from heaven. These are the images of the physical and spiritual heritage of man. Christ flows through the whole tree like sap, and we who are in Christ flow through it too in him. It is in this dimension that intercession becomes valid and finds its raison d'etre—not in remembering long lists of names but by uniting the self in a two-way movement which is always going on. It is a witness at once to the solidarity of man and to the uniqueness of every man, to the solidarity of the whole mystical body of Christ and to the uniqueness of Christ. Within the prayer of intercession these things must be held together. We pray, 'Jesus Christ, Son of the Living God, have mercy upon us.' Jesus Christ, present in this person who has been injured by mankind's sin which is my sin, have mercy upon us. Have mercy because we have tarnished the work of your hands by sectarianism, by indifference, by fear. If we have done these things to another, even though not to the one for whom we are praying, he too is within the tree, he is not unharmed. But at the same time we say, Jesus Christ, transcendent God, unique Lord of the universe through whom all things were made, have mercy on this person who is not innocent, who has himself sinned in his relationship with God, with others and towards himself, who has himself made wounds within the body of Christ. Whatever form of words or silence is used, every man is at one and the same time Christ being persecuted by mankind and the powers of darkness, and the one who is himself persecuting Christ. Between these two focal points of intercession everything essential which can happen to the one for whom we pray is comprehended.

Yet below this movement, enfolding and quickening it, must be the affirmation of obedience to things as they are. We must say, 'Jesus Christ, Son of God, hallowed be thy Name' across the world, animate and inanimate, as it comes to us through time and space. Through the authority given to Adam in the beginning, and reaffirmed when Christ arose out of hell, we can bless the world so that, within that blessing, it can find its true life and function in the whole order of being. Only so can it become an instrument of ultimate good, even though for many of us, for much of the time, its face may seem to be dark and terrible or—what is perhaps worse—grey, monotonous and meaningless.

The responsibility to work for reconciliation which communities take upon themselves when they dare to risk living in an enclosed situation is not only carried out through their prayer but also through their existential acts. The only thing which binds together a group of people, diverse as mankind itself, is the spiritual vision of vocation. But this does not absolve them on the horizontal level from the tensions involved in diversity of colour, of race, of natural gifts, of educational opportunity, of age, of temperament, of the thousand differences which can either fragment a community or provide the raw material for a reconciliation and spiritual unity which will spread far beyond the geographical limits of its own home to those whom it will never see or know in this life.

Every man, every community, sums up history at a single point, containing as each one does not only particular experiences and memories but the common emotions and wounds of all mankind. Within a community the occasions for the eruptions of these things may seem to be small and trivial, yet the raw stuff of humanity which is revealed through them is identical to that which produces wars between nations, discrimination and persecution among groups of men. Somewhere, sometime, there have to be those who will stand and refuse to allow the dreary succession of cause and effect to continue, absorbing the evil as Christ did on the cross, because of their incorporation in him. For us it is rarely a matter of heroics but more often of some infinitesimal detail, which nevertheless is the hair's breadth separating the spiral of love stretching up and out to infinity, from the spiral of destruction which drags man down into that vortex out of which springs the next consequence of sin. Christians too often think that they are called to escape from evil, and at times there may have to be a temporary strategy of retreat, but in fact the healing comes from within the heart of evil itself as it is absorbed by a person or a group whose will is steadily set towards God in worship and trust. There is a painting by El Greco which illustrates an apocryphal incident in the life of St. John the Divine. In his hand he holds the Chalice within which is coiled a small

fiery dragon. The cup of Gethsemane, the cup of communion, contains
poison, and it is in the drinking of it that the greatest evil becomes the
greatest good.

However, there is a vocation to Christian protest as there is to Christian
acceptance; but this is of little value unless it arises out of an inner con-
frontation with evil. It is even less valid if protest against outward abuses
is used as an alternative to, or an escape from, personal responsibility. The
Elder Zossima's words in *The Brothers Karamazov* may seem exaggerated,
yet they contain the kernel of the truth out of which compassionate and
dispassionate protest must spring:

'If the evil-doing of men moves you to indignation and overwhelming
distress, even to a desire for vengeance on the evil-doers, shun above all
things that feeling. Go at once and seek suffering for yourself, as though
you were yourself guilty of that wrong. Accept that suffering and bear it
and your heart will find comfort, and you will understand that you too are
guilty . . .'

The 'horizontal' witness of the contemplative community

By its very existence community life faces some of the greatest problems
of human relationships, namely, how to balance the claims of the corporate
with those of the individual; how to balance an extroversion and an intro-
version, either of which carried to excess, could rob a community or an
individual of its particular character and personality; how to balance the
individual's unique relationship to God with the corporate spiritual ideals
and the working out of them in the common life; how to balance eternal
truth with the sociological and psychological insights of the age into which
the community is born.

Although through the seventeen centuries of Christian monastic life
there have been many misunderstandings and abuses, yet the ancient Rules,
from which modern communities take their inspiration, are all based on
principles of justice and charity which have to be worked for, and worked
in the temporal order. So a community, if it is to be relevant, must always
be alert and on the move, with a movement which is not haphazard nor
undertaken for the sake of modernity, but one which is a genuine expression for the twentieth century of truths which are unchangeable in
themselves. Traditional disciplines which have stood the test of the years
do not have to be abandoned, but it is necessary to re-examine their

context and meaning so that they can speak with a living voice to those who come either to join the community or to visit it.

The witness of silence

Silence in its Godward aspect is a necessary condition for a life of prayer. Yet in its human orientation there are those who find no purpose in it today, and these sometimes include those older members of communities who have experienced it in the past as tending to isolation, coldness and indifference. Yet it seems that the young and the not-so-young visit religious communities today for the very purpose of discovering a silence which they cannot find elsewhere. It is the quality of silence which needs to be examined, not the fact itself. Silence and chastity are closely related. The imbalance of a century ago arose from the fear that human love in community life might detract from the love of God, and where there was fear, stiffness and coldness were the inevitable consequence. It is commonly recognised now among Religious that chastity must embrace all creaturely relationships so that we are in danger of falling into the opposite error of forgetting that it is only when there is space around each person—and indeed around each community—that a true relationship with anyone or anything becomes possible. The dignity and value of any human entity, be it corporate or individual, depends on a certain reticence which demands that everything should not be spilled out all the time. In the indignity of brain-washing and forced confessions the personality can be radically damaged. The intrusions of bugging and computerisation need to be off-set as never before by the witness of a silence which is not cold and selfish, nor based on fear, but on a delicacy of communication which is beyond words and allows the other to be. Words themselves do not break it if they are spoken out of silence when there is something meaningful to be said, and by those who, despite their own human frailty, are directed towards charity and reconciliation.

There is, of course, a very delicate balance to be maintained. Unless there is the willingness to try to give the self away existentially and not merely in theory it is possible to become like an autistic child who appears to have no personality because he cannot communicate it. So the contemplative community, with its times of silence and of recreation, of deeper withdrawal and of festival and fun, which can include within itself diverse manifestations of its spirit, bears witness to a richness of life on the horizontal level which can happen only where there is the common prayer, the common spirit, and a unity which binds all together in a charity and trust which underlies both speech and silence.

What has been said about the relationship of the individual to the community can likewise be applied to that of the community to the outside world, and this is one of the purposes of enclosure. Unless a community has space in which to work out its own particular vocation it will have nothing to offer through its openness. Again this is not a local and recent problem but one which is world-wide and historical—as may be seen in the later books of the Old Testament. Does holiness demand physical, spiritual, or cultural separation? Or does it ask for involvement in these spheres with the world of its own generation? There is no cut and dried answer. We desire security in one or other of these extremes, and there is no security except at the point of balance between contradictions. And it is only by being held at this point of balance that a community can avoid becoming fossilised, and can be capable of a discrimination which recognizes the Holy Spirit's leading in its corporate life.

Committal and the life of the Vows

In his book *Asking the Fathers* Aelred Squire makes an important point concerning the integral unity of the human person. He says:

'Tremendously important for our general spiritual development and also for our life of prayer, is the capacity to get a sense of ourselves as persisting through a whole succession of happenings . . . It is necessary to realise that one cannot live in the present moment wisely unless one has a sense of the nature and significance of previous moments. If we are so identified with what we experience in the present moment that we forget that we, in the depths of our being, are not simply and solely what we experience, then we learn nothing by living, we do not grow and we do not mature.' [1]

The discussion which is going on today on the advisability or otherwise of life-long commitment in the Religious Life hangs on this point. Is there a core of personality and therefore of vocation which persists throughout the physical, emotional and intellectual changes of one person's life-span, enabling him to live without compromise or dishonesty? This is a problem

1. P. 169. Published by SPCK 1973.

that also concerns the married state which is likewise one in which being and loving are more important than action. One might ask if love can be eternal, if there is any real value in a fidelity which persists when all feeling and meaning seem to have died. Will not the person become shrivelled, sour and prematurely old if he is tied to a life which no longer seems relevant nor gives him any joy? These are fears—whether real or imaginary—experienced by many in the Religious Life today.

The answer for the individual can only be through the vertical response which has already been discussed but, nevertheless, communities have to ask themselves whether they are demanding from their members obedience to a time-table rather than to a life. The ancient monastic Rules were large and generous in scope and ideals; it is when they are narrowed down, by fear or by a desire for security, to a series of common observances that they become incapable of containing living people. It is true that the corporate spirit has to be expressed through sacramentals of common order, but within that order there needs to be a wide scope for a variety of expressions of vocation which will give the person room to change and to grow, according to his age, his length of time in the community, and his own particular needs at any specific time. Some, for instance, may be called to a life of greater withdrawal, some to wider involvement with the outside world, some to live in smaller or larger groups, and this is something which has to be accepted if life-long commitment is to be fruitful. The community, as well as the individual, has to be obedient to the reality of things as they are, to the nature of people as they are. But the flexibility involved will not cause divisiveness if the individual is concerned primarily not with his own self-interest, but with making the fullest contribution that he can to the life and work of his community at any given time.

What then do the Vows of poverty, chastity and obedience involve? If they are defined in some intellectual way this may give the reason for their existence but does not convey the existential experience of them in the life of a twentieth century community or of individuals within it. For the community a realistic poverty involves simplicity, a moderation which recognizes the need to possess enough money in the bank to support a number of persons who have ceased to pay their Social Security contributions, enough to maintain monastic buildings which are suitable for their purpose, a certain amount for emergencies, but no more. Corporate spiritual poverty implies a recognition of the need for flexibility, readiness to respond to the leadings of the Holy Spirit, not too much care about one's reputation, not too much worldly wisdom. For the individual Religious, poverty as it is experienced along the line of life usually reveals itself as an invitation to let something go, a particular work or something which seems essential for it, a cherished opinion, a blockage of unforgiveness. It is non-material possessions which are clung to most tenaciously since the greater good for which they are to be dropped rarely reveals itself until the act of letting go has been accomplished.

Chastity—the whole being set on God—grows through a developing experience of prayer. There are certain things which can be said about personal, contemplative prayer and these have been enunciated by the great masters of the spiritual life throughout the centuries. Yet even they cannot pin down the Holy Spirit's action on any individual life in words or formulae. The saints and doctors of the Church have given us maps of the way, yet the map cannot be read accurately until one has had some personal experience of the terrain and of the difficulties of climbing. There are well-known, well-tried methods of preparation for prayer involving the reason, the imagination and the will, many of which seem irrelevant today. More relevant perhaps are the techniques drawn from Eastern religions which help to prepare the body as an entity for God's work upon the whole man. For the thread which binds together every experience of prayer is an increasingly pure chastity of intention whereby all things, within and without, are being brought to God in a simple act of worship, acceptance and penitence. In this simplicity of relationship anything may and will happen for there are no blue-prints for the action of the Holy Spirit upon a life which is open to his leading.

Obedience, as was said earlier, must involve the acceptance of the greatest amount of total reality that we are capable of at any given time. For the Religious this involves among other things a framework, a hierarchical order which many communities today are attempting to abandon, feeling that it has nothing to offer to a twentieth century conception of community life. Yet, within the whole Religious Life, the contemplative community in particular is witnessing not only to present insights but to the tradition out of which it has grown, to a history which cannot be abandoned. Some are more temperamentally attracted to ritual than others, yet there is no dense, important form of human community, whether it be national, political or ecclesiastical, which has not its own forms of ritual, binding the past to the present, with the total experience giving weight and meaning to the ephemeral and temporal. Once ritual is abandoned something essential tends to disintegrate too. This is true of Christian community, which is an expression of obedience to traditional as well as to immediate and pentecostal experience.

The adult, in contrast to the child, has learnt that all reality cannot be encountered at once; it is too vast and too terrifying. But he acknowledges and accepts total reality in intention through symbols, sacraments and rituals which, nevertheless, must not be allowed to lose touch with the reality which they express. Then when the actual cup of sacrifice is offered to any life it is more likely to be recognised and accepted for what it is—an experience through living flesh, nerves and blood of the same reality which was known sacramentally through a hundred acts of communion.

Conclusion

It will be seen that the witness of the life of a contemplative community is of a balanced kind, working out in unspectacular and humble ways the implications and consequences of many of today's problems, It is part of the witness that the fruits of these experiments in living should be communicated, through the spoken and written word, in a flexible openness, to those who come to visit it. This is always a two-way exchange for no one community can presume to think that it has nothing to learn from the rest of the Church or from the world as a whole. Sometimes the exchange may involve individuals going out of enclosure for longer or shorter periods for specific reasons, in order to study, for example, or for ecumenical purposes. This is in the tradition of the Fathers of the desert whose normal rule of stability in one place did not exclude visits to Alexandria or to each other as need arose, or charity demanded.

So the contemplative community witnesses to the two great commandments of love of God and love of neighbour worked out in a particular form of life which will differ in details and orientation between one community and another. Because the results of such a vocation are not pragmatic and material, and can only be measured in terms of conversion of life, it will always remain something of a scandal to an activist world. Yet today when that world stands helpless before a mystery of evil, which it seems unable to understand or to transform, there are many who see hope only in inner self-giving to a spiritual warfare whose scope we cannot measure, whose depth we cannot fathom, but which nevertheless seems the most relevant and important thing in life. God is sovereign over all being, but in this twisted world he has to be affirmed to be so. God has conquered evil, but the victory has to be made meaningful in each generation through the living flesh and blood of his members. God is continually creating and recreating the world, yet the world must be open to his action if it is to be renewed and divinised.

It is to facts such as these, intangible and known only to faith, that the contemplative life witnesses, and which the contemplative community incarnates on its own spot of earth and in its own span of time. And it is within this milieu that the 'science of love' can be worked out fruitfully within and for the Church and the world.